Working in Canadian Communities
JOBS IN RURAL CANADA

BY TODD KORTEMEIER

True North is published by Beech Street Books
27 Stewart Rd. Collingwood, ON Canada L9Y 4M7

www.beechstreetbooks.ca

Produced by Red Line Editorial

Photographs ©: BGSmith/Shutterstock Images, cover, 1; Sophia Granchinho/Shutterstock Images, 4–5; Benoit Daoust/
Shutterstock Images, 6; LaiQuocAnh/Shutterstock Images, 8–9; Andrew Park/Shutterstock Images, 10–11; Kevin Brine/
Shutterstock Images, 12–13; Photographee.eu/Shutterstock Images, 14–15; Sergey_R/Shutterstock Images, 16–17; Alex533/
Shutterstock Images, 18–19; Red Line Editorial, 20–21

Editor: Heather C. Hudak
Designer: Laura Polzin

Library and Archives Canada Cataloguing in Publication

Kortemeier, Todd, 1986-, author
        Jobs in rural Canada / by Todd Kortemeier.

(Working in Canadian communities)
Includes bibliographical references and index.
Issued in print and electronic formats.
ISBN 978-1-77308-025-3 (hardback).--ISBN 978-1-77308-053-6
(paperback).--ISBN 978-1-77308-081-9 (pdf).--ISBN 978-1-77308-109-0
(html)

        1. Occupations--Canada--Juvenile literature. 2. Country
life--Canada--Juvenile literature. I. Title.

HF5382.5.C2K6 2016   j331.700971   C2016-903602-2
                                             C2016-903603-0

Printed in the United States of America
Mankato, MN
August 2016

TABLE OF CONTENTS

Chapter One

NATURAL RESOURCE JOBS

Canada has many natural resources. These materials are made naturally by the Earth. Forests and **minerals** are natural resources. Millions of Canadians work in natural resources jobs. Many of these jobs are in rural areas. Rural areas are places that have fewer than 1,000 people living in them. There are fewer than 400 people per square kilometre of land.

Canada has many forests. People work in forestry jobs in all parts of Canada, except Nunavut. There are very few forests in Nunavut.

Many rural areas depend on forestry jobs to make money. Some people cut down trees. The wood is used

Baker Lake is a community in the Kivalliq region of Nunavut.

MINING COMMUNITIES

Canada is rich in natural minerals. Tonnes of gold, iron **ore**, and lead are mined each year. Most mines are rural. People often travel a long way to reach mines. The Diavik Diamond Mine is 300 kilometres northeast of Yellowknife, Northwest Territories. The Arctic Circle is only approximately 220 kilometres away. Often, people live on the mine site while working. This keeps them from travelling long distances home every day.

Some forestry workers use chainsaws to cut down trees.

to make many products. It may be used to build houses or fences.

Forestry work is more than just cutting down trees. **Biologists** find the best places to cut down trees. They test the soil. Some people drive big trucks to haul away the trees. Mechanics make sure the trucks and other machines are in good working order. People who work at **saw mills** cut trees into lumber. Workers at paper mills turn wood into paper. Every Canadian province has at least one type of mill. Aboriginal Peoples help find ways to protect the land.

Quebec, British Columbia, and Ontario have the most forestry jobs in Canada. New Brunswick has some of the most rural areas in Canada. There, more than 15,000 people work in forestry. That's small compared to other provinces. But it's a lot for New Brunswick's small population. Almost everyone in New Brunswick knows someone who works in forestry.

KEEPING FORESTS SAFE

Deforestation happens when a forest is completely cut down. Workers take steps to make sure Canada's forests remain healthy. Companies can only cut down a certain number of trees. They have workers who plant seedlings so new trees grow. Only a very small number of forests have been deforested.

Chapter Two

FARMING JOBS

Nearly 300,000 Canadians work in farming jobs. They do many types of jobs. Some farmers grow crops. They may also raise animals, such as cows and pigs. Each province and territory has a part in Canada's farming industry. Farmers in Quebec raise cows for milk. Foods from rural Canada are sent across the country. Some are even sent around the world.

Almost all farms in Canada are in rural areas. They take up a lot of space. In central Alberta, the average farm size is more than three square kilometres. Rural Red Deer County has the best farming in the region. Farmers here raise chickens and grow **barley**.

A farm in rural Alberta

8

JOBS ON THE FARM

Farmers have a big job to do. If they raise animals, they have to feed and care for them. If they plant crops, they have to make sure they get enough water. Then they have to harvest the crops at the end of the season. Most farms have workers to get the job done. Some people drive equipment to harvest crops. **Veterinarians** make sure animals stay healthy. Truck drivers help drive the goods to market.

British Columbia's Okanagan Valley is known for its fruit. There are thousands of fruit farms. Many rural Canadians work here. They grow and pick cherries, grapes, and apples.

Farmers take their wheat to massive grain elevators after harvest.

Chapter Three

MANUFACTURING JOBS

Rural Canada has a lot of space for manufacturing. Factories take up a large amount of land. Manufacturing is huge in Canada. More than 1.7 million Canadians work in the industry. All types of products are made in Canada. Most manufacturing is located in Ontario and Quebec. Many people here build cars.

Engineers design the cars. Other workers build them. Some put the car's engine together. Others shape the body of the car. These workers need a lot of training.

Factories have a lot of different jobs. Some people work on an **assembly line**. They put products together.

A concrete factory in Pleasant Valley, New Brunswick

In big factories, people drive equipment to move parts from place to place. Other people work in the offices. They sell the products to people around the world. People load the products onto trucks. Drivers take them to stores. They may also take them to ports or railways. Here they are shipped to faraway places.

Assembly-line workers often do the same task all day long.

Chapter Four

ENERGY JOBS

Some of Canada's natural resources are hidden. They are underground in remote, rural areas. One of Canada's biggest resources is oil. Canada is the fifth-largest oil producer in the world. Hundreds of thousands of Canadians work in oil.

Alberta has more oil than any other province. It has more oil than some countries. About 130,000 people work in oil jobs in Alberta. Most oil is found on land in rural Alberta.

There are many types of oil jobs. Some people drill the oil from the ground. Others **maintain** the equipment. Some people work on **pipelines**. These pipes, as well as

Workers constructing a pipeline

16

OIL USES

More than 200,000 Canadians work in oil and gas. Oil is used in other industries in Canada. It is used to make gasoline. It is also used in **pavement** for roads. It heats homes and businesses.

trains and trucks, take the oil to the places where it will be used. Scientists and engineers help find the oil. They also come up with ways to get it out of the ground. There also are many managers on site. They help the whole team run smoothly.

Many rural Canadians work in the natural gas industry. Natural gas is an energy source. It is found inside rocks. It provides a third of Canada's energy needs. Workers have to drill into the ground to find the gas. Every province and territory except Nunavut has natural gas workers. This is because it is difficult to get at the natural gas in Nunavut.

GETTING THE GAS

There are many natural gas companies in British Columbia. Rural areas outside small towns, such as Kitimat and Prince Rupert, have natural gas plants. **Geologists** find out which rocks have gas inside. Some workers use drills to get at the gas. Others work on pipelines. Truck drivers haul equipment to bigger towns.

Burrard Inlet in British Columbia is home to an oil refinery.

19

A RURAL COMMUNITY

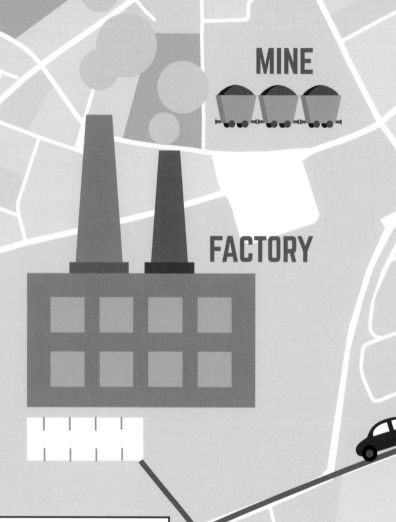

MINE

FACTORY

1 CM = 0.5 KM

— = ROUTE TO WORK

N W E S

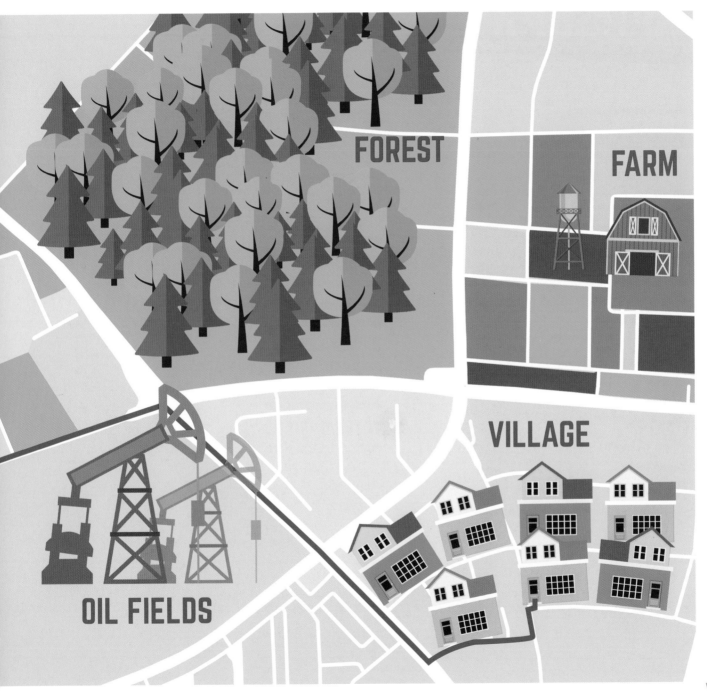

FOREST

FARM

VILLAGE

OIL FIELDS

21

GLOSSARY

ASSEMBLY LINE
a lineup of machines and people in a factory who each build a part of an object

BARLEY
a crop grown for use in food

BIOLOGISTS
scientists who study living things

GEOLOGISTS
scientists who study natural features, such as rocks

MAINTAIN
the act of caring for machinery or property

MINERALS
natural materials obtained by mining

ORE
natural minerals or rocks that are made of metal

PAVEMENT
material used to cover roads and sidewalks

PIPELINES
long pipes that are used to transport substances, such as oil, over long distances

SAW MILLS
places designed to cut trees into small, usable pieces

VETERINARIANS
doctors for animals

TO LEARN MORE

BOOKS

Dickmann, Nancy. *Jobs on a Farm*. Chicago: Heinemann Library, 2011.

Marsico, Katie. *Working at a Factory*. Ann Arbor, MI: Cherry Lake Publishing, 2009.

Miller, Mirella. *Oil Worker*. Mankato, MN: Child's World, 2015.

WEBSITES

CANADIAN FORESTRY ASSOCIATION: KIDS' CORNER
http://canadianforestry.com/wp/kids-corner

KNOWITALL.ORG: EXPLORING CAREERS
http://media.knowitall.org/series/career-aisle-career-clusters

NATURAL RESOURCES CANADA: WELCOME TO THE KIDS' CLUB
http://www.nrcan.gc.ca/energy/efficiency/kidsclub/7805

INDEX

ABOUT THE AUTHOR

Todd Kortemeier is a journalist, an editor, and a children's book author. He has authored dozens of books for young people on a wide variety of topics.

24